# All That Glitters From The Mind Of A Poet Is Not Gold!

David L. Anderson

Foreword by Pamela Norris

Preparation for publishing by Pamela Norris
This book was published posthumously

This book was printed in the United States of America

ISBN-13: 9781797042770

Contact and Order Information:
email: artsypoetry101@gmail.com
http://www.Amazon.com

# DEDICATION

To all of my friends, family, and extended family. All of whom have showed their love and support unconditionally. I thank you all and love you more than words can express.

David Lamont Anderson "Divad"
September 30, 1969 – September 22, 2015

# CONTENTS

# CONTENTS

# ACKNOWLEDGMENTS

First, I acknowledge God for His unconditional love for me, and for giving me gifts of poetry and song to edify, entertain, and inspire those whom I came in contact.

I would also like to thank my friend, and my sister in the arts, Pamela Norris for her support and making this book possible.
Thanks.

# FOREWORD

I met David many moons ago when we were freshmen at Morris Brown College in Atlanta, Georgia. We lived next door to one another in student boarding houses. We instantly connected and looked out for each other. I remember the first time I heard him sing, my jaw dropped because I had never heard a more melodious voice in my life. We began singing together and sharing our song writing abilities. David was not only a gifted song writer, musician, and singer, but he was also a very skilled dancer. I remember thinking, "Damn, is there anything that he can't do?" I was proud and honored to have him as a friend and walk throughout the campus with him. He went on to pursue his music career, and later changed his name to Divad. So, from here on out, I will refer to my good friend as Divad as he requested.

Fast forward about 25 years. I convinced Divad to publish some of his writings in a book. Since I am also a poet/writer and have self published many books before, I knew that I could be a tremendous help in the process. I also knew in my heart that his writings should be shared with everyone. He has such a witty sense of expression and an incomparable way of putting his own 'spin' on words. We started working together again, this time by telephone because he lived in Georgia, and I lived in California. We agreed that he would text his poetry to me, and I would re-type them on my computer, and prepare his book for publishing.

The journey to completing this book would not be an easy one. We had a few setbacks because of his illness, but he persevered until the end. We spent the next two years getting the poetry together for his book. Originally, he was going to use many of his writings that were previously written and stored in a folder. However, the folder was misplaced and he had to write new poems.  I encouraged him that his gift will always create and to continue to write. I sent him my poetry books and he would read them and tell me which ones were his favorites. I believe that my poetry books also inspired him to write new poetry. So, instead of texting his poetry, he now had to call me and recite the new poems; and I would type them on my computer or write them down as he recited.

I was able to send him a proof copy of his book. He loved it! He only made a few minor changes. Divad was able to see our project through just days before he made his transition. There are not enough words to describe how honored I am to complete this book for Divad. I promised him that I would follow through with the changes and get his book published. He was my friend, and I will never forget the joy and companionship he brought to my life. So, with all said, I truly hope that you enjoy this compilation of poetry that Divad has selected for your enjoyment.

From The Heart Of Your Sister In The Arts;
You Were My Good Friend And Will Always
Be Remembered And Missed: For Friendship
Is Eternal.

*Pamela Norris* ©™

DAVID L. ANDERSON

# ALL THAT GLITTERS

# FROM THE MIND OF A POET IS NOT GOLD!

DAVID L. ANDERSON

# ALL THAT GLITTERS
# IS NOT GOLD

There is a mountain, and it's mighty high
You cannot reach the top
Unless you can fly

There is a molehill called a proving ground
Ain't no'where to go less you hand around
Everybody wants to tell
What's already been told
And everybody wants to sell
What's already been sold

What's the use of money
If it's only goin' to get stole
Even at the center of the fire there is cold
All that glitters ain't gold

Put this together
And it shall make sense to you

◆ ◆ ◆

# AS I LAY AWAKE ON MY DEATH BED

I could hardly hear the words that you said
The sky seems so dark to me
Without my glasses I can still see
The lovely blouse you wore just for me
I smell the scent of your sweet perfume
It gently fills the hospital room

The doctor told me that it won't be long
Before I will be walking and singing
My own song
I have seen the way that you can do
What the doctor said I can tell that it is true

If you believe in Christ and so will you too
Not to say that you will raise the dead
The power comes from the Lord
So listen to what He says

Everything in prayer gets deep into your soul
That's the only way you can be whole
This is a message that He gave to you
Just as the night is black
And the morning sky is blue

♦♦♦

# CAN I SEE YOUR FUNNY FACE?

Can I see that face you make
When we be making love?
The sound like the heavens from up above
So we toss and turn and I really want to learn
More of the feelings that I feel for you

Do you know what I'm thinking of?
Want to see that funny face you make?
The breath on your neck is when
I am just trying to test those living waters
That comes flowing from your love

You gently take from me what you can
Already know that I am your man
So let us stop playing these silly games
Cause you know just who I am

♦ ♦ ♦

# CASMIR

Met this dude and his name was Casmir
He didn't talk much first thing he said
To me was, "Yo, you come here."

I was stunned by the offer
But turned on by his tone
But the look on his face said
He didn't want to be alone

So I went straight over to him
And I looked him in his face
Then I plucked his button
On his nice crisp shirt
I saw that bulge in his jeans
Slowly go down a smerch

♦ ♦ ♦

# COME ALONG MY CHILDREN

Come along my children,
Come and sing this song
It's all about the way you live
And the things that can go wrong

Come along my children,
We need to be aware
To get a chance of happiness
If you show them that you care

Come along my children,
It's time to stop playing games
Just because you are children,
Doesn't mean you can't make a new way

Come along my children;
Is it true that the time has come?
When the Lord Jesus is going to come
And the apocalypse is begun

Have we been so naughty
And the nice people that live just right?
We hope that we can save our souls
By the end of this night
I can see the rain of fire
And the clouds are not far behind

We must get busy saving souls
So the battle they can fight
God has fully prepared us for
This day that is to come
If you have not given him your soul,
Then I mourn for you my chum

I think I know a secret
To where you can be with God
Take all your material things
And give 'em all back to them
No matter what happens to you
Never turn your back on Him

Good night to all the sinners
Who think they've won the war
For they cannot know
What Jesus has planned
For the true believers forevermore
Praise God now and save your soul right now
It's just that simple we've won the war

♦ ♦ ♦

# COME AROUND HERE

Never wanted to tell you what to do
Even though I am in love with you
Even though I doubt the truth in you
Whenever you come around here

◆ ◆ ◆

# DO YOU REMEMBER

Do you remember
When we did not get along?
And I knew that you
Would be special everyday

You are such a spicy singer
Because you put me through the ringer
By twisting my mind and giving me the finger

On the first day of September
When you told me "no"
All my friends said to me,
"Didn't we tell you so?"
They said that, "We even warned your ass
but then you go on ahead
and do what you want to do"

Something always happens
And I will be the one to say
what did I tell you?

♦ ♦ ♦

# FILL THE WORLD
# WITH LOVE

Come take my hand and see the land
Where no one dies for the pride of their flag
Come take my hand my brothers
And come see the land of the free

When a gun is fired in your nightmares
And you can smell the stale smoke in the air
Let's make a world for our children
So they don't grow old
With the blood of war on their hands

Somebody tell me, why we are fighting?
War is not an exchange for blood
If we could build a patriot missile
We can fill the world with love

Come dry my tears and ease my fears
Cause a lover of mine
Lost his life just last year
When this storm blows,
Will pollution air free flow?
Then someone tell me, please
What we gain from the casualties?

Somebody tell me, why we are fighting?
War is not an exchange for blood
If Bush could build a patriot missile
We can fill the world with love

◆ ◆ ◆

# HE SPOKE TO ME

In the middle of the day
It was then that I heard him say
"You are not alone in this world,
For I shall always be with you"

I couldn't even make a sound
Cause my life was upside down
And everybody knew that there was
Something that I was going through

At the time of this test
I really wanted to get some rest
But most unlikely to do
That I would fail

I look down at my watch
I saw the time that I forgot to be a person
Who could do most anything

♦ ♦ ♦

# I SAW YOU PEEKING

I was walking down the street
Looking at my feet
Wishing that I had something else to do
Then my phone in my pocket went off
I had to dig down deep and quick before
The caller got to sick of waiting for
Me to pick it up

How glad I was to hear
My old friend Larry's voice in my ear
Cause the last time that we spoke
I told him how I wanted him to choke
And it was not so pleasant,
Not the way I wanted him to go

This was a snip to get us gone from the "T"
That we all love to be inside
Their plan went through but what can I do
Now what is there to do?

Yo, I was not trying to kill my buddy by far
We'd been together for many years
And killing wouldn't be great for me at all
He is too a pal and confidant
It would be too much for me
Love him too much
For me to be a few months
And a friend of mine is what I can see for me

The place shall be - I will be

A smile on my face and then your place
To have a few people who are ready to
Because I can get it for my selfish
To play them for myself

♦ ♦ ♦

# I THOUGHT I WAS GOING TO DIE

Should it be my place for me to say
That I will know the day
In which I would go away from
The earth in any way?

So I sit and count the days of my demise
And is it really to my surprise
To see that I am still alive?
When everyone has said to me
That I would not see
But the good Lord has a different way for me

I have been here too long to say
The intended time I'd go away
And not until the master says
That it's time for me to come his way

I feel so glad today
That I have more time for me to pray
To the God of my understanding
Each and every day

♦ ♦ ♦

# I'M HURT

Been a long time since
I've written down a line
Still inspirations escapes my mind
Ever since I lost a little part of me
She was a sweet little girl of eighteen
She was way too young for her
To ever leave the scene

She left her mama, her daddy,
And her baby all alone
We all were wondering,
"Where the hell did it go wrong?"
Then a voice had answered us that
God had took her home

So, I mourn a little longer
And I'll grow a little stronger
And hope of my family I pray to grow
Forever longer with Roman
He makes us all remember his mother
The only son, I know that he is the me
That I always wanted to be

♦ ♦ ♦

# IT SEEMS TO ME

It seems to me as I laugh and cry
That it really don't seem to matter
Whether I live or die
The rain will still fall on all of us
All over even if we try to stay dry
We get wet inside
We all need to be a culture
That lives and thrive
Not upon one another, but together
It's not a hard thing to do
It's like tying your shoe
Or like the lady sings the blues
And like a heart that is true
Or like saying, "I love you"

It seems to me that we all have a part to do
In this scheme of life
To love one another
That is what Jesus told us to do
It was his last words and from that point on
When someone has a final request
It is usually carried out
But in this case and at this time
People honor nothing and want nothing
But material things

It makes me angry to see how these
Teens are killing their parents

With no regard, and turn around
And kill their own selves
Ensuring their place in the devil's arms
Satan is on the rise
And I'm surprised
I saw it in my very own eyes ten years ago
And now it's true

♦ ♦ ♦

# LOVE CAN'T LEAVE

Love can't leave you alone
Unless you open the door
A chance for love like this
May not come anymore
But if you hold on to things that you hope for
Our love will be brand new

Love can't leave
I tried so hard to let you know that
Love can't leave

Sometimes when I am by myself
I realized how it felt
When you would hold me tight
Hold tight with all your might
I know if I could just hold you
Our love would be brand new

LOVE CAN'T LEAVE!
I want you to know that

♦ ♦ ♦

# LOVE YOU TO THE NINE

Would you hug me on a crowded street?
Would you keep your cool
If washed your feet?
And your soul a bath, what if I gave it?
And your body, I add,
How long would you save it?

Would you lie down on a bed of thorns
As I drink your ocean dry?
If I told you that I loved you
Instead of laughing would you cry?

Could you kiss three times
With your dress upside down
Stroking and laughing
Would you lay awake for 14 hours
Listening to the grass grow

Now tell me...
Could you, would you love me to the nine?
Could you love me for all time?
Could you love me to the nine?

♦ ♦ ♦

# MY BLACK WOMAN

She was my mom, my sister,
My niece, or grand mother
But she was a woman...
A wonderful black woman

I saw her get smacked down to the floor
And he was going to jail for that
If I can help it

But she won't press charges cause
She didn't want to see him in jail
All I can say is, "What the hell?"

◆ ◆ ◆

DAVID L. ANDERSON

# MY VOICE

When you know what you know
That the day is going to come
When you are not
Using it for a good reason

Why are you going back to the place
Where you didn't have a voice?
I'm not going back there
To that silent room
I have been there too long ago
And now it's time for me to speak out
And say something to someone

You are that someone
I just hope that you can embrace it
And hold on to it
For we may never have this time again

♦ ♦ ♦

# ONE FINE DAY

One fine day the birds were singing
And love was in the air that I could touch
Was it the fourth of July or was it all just a lie
I was trying to figure out which one

Well to tell you the truth
I went and sat on the roof
To sit and ponder a way that I should poof

I really like the way that it smells
It's just like the some sauce that
I used to cook
I only like burned very well

So like a kite I am high
As I look at the sky
And I laugh at the people
As they go walking by
Wonder where they are going
Seems like my high is flowing
And I know where I'm going
I think I should have another pull
From my tree
I ain't trying to fall but
I am a little too high to avoid it

On this fine ass day
Can you dig it?

♦ ♦ ♦

# ONE MORE DAY

Thank you Lord for...This is the day that
The Lord had made me glad
With him being blind in all this
He poured his heart out
But He never mentioned
That He was The son of God,
And the brother of man

Those who knew Him not will indeed perish
Those who were ignorant will be spared
For He was not a man that He could lie
However, the Pharisee told Him
That He will die telling them their own truth
He wanted them to pass this down
To the youth while they grew
So they'd know of the name of Jesus

Even though they beat Him
And spat upon His face
Instead of cursing them
He asked of His Father to forgive them
Because they know not what they do
Then my savior Jesus Christ
Hung His head  down and then he died

I still can't comprehend why
After all that He had done
That they did not see that He was the one
They have been waiting for
He was a man that walks in the truth

Because he was the light of man
My heart breaks when I hear
The story of His crucifixion
I almost fall apart

♦ ♦ ♦

# OPEN YOUR MIND TO THIS

Back in the day,
The dudes used to say this before
They stepped in closer to get a kiss
"No" would be the word
That he's already heard
So his feelings are hurt
And his dick's in the dirt
But "no" has never been said
He turns quickly and away in anger
Was all in his face

♦ ♦ ♦

# THE WORLD END

When you started laughing
And the sun turns black
The trees full of whispers
And the purple sky crack

Now it's too late to negotiate
Because the two major countries
Were so full of hate

As the mushroom cloud
Rose above the sky
The people down below
Knew it was time to die

Then there was an explosion
An explosion so loud
Then hot ashes fell
From the mushroom cloud

The screams on earth of horror
Were very, very short
Because the president pressed the button
Just for the sport
The End

♦♦♦

# THROUGH GOD'S EYES

When I see you I am looking at perfection
Nothing can stop my affection
Living this love is the way
We should be thinking of the action

We are all God's children
For we need not seek
I know that He is the bold
And we are the weak

I so love the Lord
He took away my tears
And I know He will be with me
Until the end of my years
I know cause I can only see you
Through the eyes of God

♦ ♦ ♦

# TIME

When we talk about wasting time
What are we really saying?
I mean how we waste something
That we don't really own

We can't possibly own time...
Some people are so rich,
They feel like their time is too expensive
For you to waste their time with them

Huh, what about God?
Would He feel the same way?
Do you think that God would feel that way?
I think not and be the same God that I know

♦ ♦ ♦

DAVID L. ANDERSON

# TO WHOM THIS MAY CONCERN

This letter is a note of sorts
Of book reports and basketball shorts
The highs and lows
The way my life goes
Round and round as my heart beats
I leave most of my heart out on the streets
To follow crows
For whatever they know
They leave us the crumbs
To behold the bums
That loves us as one
To be or become

A little boy cried at the rise of the sun
But he's done
He's dried his eyes
And wonders why
The old man quivers
The old man stands up to deliver
That letter to the nation's creation
Please change the station
To the hungry masses
That longs for classes
But stand in line for cheese from our Gov
They can't know love
From that rubber glove
Bend over, they are constantly

Raped at the gate
Where they can never enter,
Forever standing in wait
For that new day coming

Turn the page
in your morning news paper
See how Bush took off with caper
Believing his lies from the beginning of time
Fast forward, rewind

Slaves of the new corporation,
With no hesitation,
Kill the babies of wise
And my God, my God they despise
Because he's old, older than seasons
But they listen to reason
But the question still stands asking,
"Why do we make the widows cry?"
We must be the terrorists here,
We pollute the sky
From the wet to the dry
Oil spills kill the fish that we fry
So get high and forget to tie dye
Because this new revolution color is green

Gore started that scene
Where he spoke of the glacier
He said we spent too much paper
We should learn to taper
Our gross interpretation
The oil inflation –

That cause I'm not willing to die for
Turn out your lights because energy
Ain't cheap no more

One energy bulb is a dollar four
Yo' tell your people to hit the floor
Cause there's a hold up in this grocery store
See, they came to steal the present back
But in the future,
WalMart makes the others fall
But the game has been fixed
Cause they own them all

I'm like Michael, I'm "Off the Wall"
Injustice sells on every floor
In every store,
Quick lock all your doors
Cause it's spreading
No one's gonna leave here alive
We be stuck like bees in a honey hive

We try and hide our faces
When we come in these places
Looking for sales
When our souls should be free
Look at what they've done to 'we'
The end is near and inevitable and only
To whom this may concern

♦ ♦ ♦

# UNENTITLED

I know now that time is so precious
And we only have today
If I could only see the present as
The gift as what it is
We'd be able to grasp it in the moment
And cherish it 'til tomorrow
It would never go away
I am seeing a new me from what I experience
The way of the future is now,
And my past was then

Each morning when I wake up early,
I have hope for a new direction
No matter what may come
God is the conductor of my life
And He is...He just is
Forevermore, amen

You have been through a lot
These past few weeks
I get it
I am not selfish in that way
So I understand because y'all
Have been doing  and going,
Trying to keep track of your lives
Plus all the while looking out for a baby boy
You guys are Awesome and I want y'all to
know That NOW get some rest and

remember that
I have love for you all
The good, the bad, and the ugly
Parts of our lives

◆ ◆ ◆

# WHEN THE WIND BLEW IN HER HAIR

Felix touched her face
And her hair was out of place
But she was the one who acted like
His hands were on fire
She gave out such a shout saying,
"Why don't you cut it out?"

Then something happened...

And everyone saw her hair was not her hair
And in fact she was bald

♦ ♦ ♦

# ABOUT
# THE AUTHOR

# ABOUT THE AUTHOR

David Anderson was born in Plainfield, New Jersey. He resided in Riverdale, Georgia, where he also attended Morris Brown College. He began singing, composing songs, and writing poetry at an early age. He was inspired by one of his grade school teachers to use his gift of song to become all that he could become. He later pursued a recording contract as a part of the '90's boy band, The Taste, where their success was mainly experienced overseas. He has performed and shared his artistry nationally and internationally. He has also served as a youth counselor, and minister of music.

David loves to celebrate the art within him, and believes that those in the arts are surely connected and often refers to fellow artists as "brothers and sisters in the arts." His music and poetry is straightforward, inspiring, and thought provoking. He says, "I always give the glory and honor to God because He has blessed me with precious gifts so that I can share them with the world."

He was a singer, songwriter, musician, and author of All That Glitters From The Mind Of A Poet Is Not Gold. His witty spin on words of love and life topics will surely stimulate the reader's mind. David touched the hearts of his relatives, close friends, and all he came in contact with. Now he leaves this book to touch the world with his artistic expressions.

# David L. Anderson

(September 30, 1969 – September 22, 2015)

All That Glitters From The Mind Of A Poet Is Not Gold!

41